Approved Lists of Books for Rural Libraries

EDUCATIONAL BULLETIN XXVI

APPROVED LISTS OF BOOKS FOR RURAL LIBRARIES

SELECTED BY

J. Y. JOYNER

State Superintendent of Public Instruction

WITH

ANNOTATIONS AND NOTES

AND

SUGGESTIONS FOR THE CARE AND USE OF THE RURAL SCHOOL LIBRARIES

BY

MINNIE W. LEATHERMAN

Secretary Library Commission of North Carolina

ISSUED FROM THE OFFICE OF
STATE SUPERINTENDENT OF PUBLIC INSTRUCTION
RALEIGH
1916

INTRODUCTION

The plan of selecting the books for the rural libraries has been changed. The libraries will be handled as units rather than having a long list of books submitted from which to select a library. There are many reasons for this change, some of which are as follows: Under the old plan, it was impossible for our dealers to handle the books promptly and in a way that was satisfactory either to them or their patrons. Better balanced libraries will be secured when the books have been selected by an experienced librarian and an expert than when selected by people who have had less opportunity and less time to consider the matter.

The present plan: Two "original" libraries costing $30 each and three "supplemental" libraries costing $15 each have been selected. The author, title, publisher, and publishers' list prices are given. It is exceedingly important that the books be furnished in the editions specified, and purchasers are warned against inferior editions with poor binding and type unfit for children's use. Alfred Williams & Co. and The Thompson Publishing Company have placed in the office of the State Superintendent of Public Instruction all the books on these lists, showing the editions specified and guaranteeing to furnish the same to all schools ordering them. They agree that all the books furnished by them shall be equal in all respects to the samples filed.

Schools that have secured libraries heretofore and wish to order a supplemental library should order Supplemental Library, No. 3. Those which have not yet secured a library should order Original Library, No. 1 or No. 2. If No. 1 is ordered, and a supplemental library is ordered later for the same district, Supplemental Library, No. 1, should be taken; and likewise Supplemental Library, No. 2, should go with Original No. 2. The libraries have been selected in such way that Original Library, No. 1, and Supplemental Library, No. 1, form a well balanced library when combined, and likewise with Original and Supplemental, No. 2. Furthermore, when the four libraries are combined they make a well balanced library. It is hoped that many of the districts will endeavor to secure the four.

The lists of books were submitted to several out-of-State dealers, as well as to our own dealers. The lowest prices obtained were those quoted by The Thompson Publishing Company, Mr. Charles J. Parker, manager, and Alfred Williams & Co., Mr. Alfred Williams, manager, both of Raleigh. These companies have agreed to keep on hand and ship promptly the libraries on the following conditions:

(1) That cash shall accompany order.

(2) That no premiums shall be offered.

(3) That library shall be shipped as a unit.

(4) That they shall be sole distributors.

It is therefore earnestly requested that these conditions be complied with in the ordering of the libraries.

Miss Minnie W. Leatherman, Secretary of the North Carolina Library Commission, has rendered valuable assistance in helping to select the books for the "Approved Lists of Books." At our request she prepared this bulletin on the care and use of the school library. We wish to express our appreciation of her valuable services.

J. Y. JOYNER,

E. E. SAMS,   *State Superintendent of Public Instruction.*

Library Clerk.

CONTENTS

SUGGESTIONS TO LIBRARIANS

1. Checking up the Library

As soon as a library is received check up the books with the proper list. This checking up is very important and if carefully done will show two things: First, whether or not all the books have been received, and if not, which ones are lacking. Second, whether or not the proper edition of each book has been sent.

To check up.—If Original Library No. 2 has been ordered, turn to the list of books in Original Library No. 2 on page 10 of this pamphlet. Take any book from the box, find it in the list and put a check opposite. It will be quite easy to find the books in the list as the list is arranged alphabetically by the authors' surnames. When the checking up is being done the librarian should notice whether or not the books are in perfect condition and if it is the edition of the book that is indicated in the list. Sometimes the edition or series to which a book belongs is given on the cover, sometimes on one of the first pages, and sometimes on the title page. In every case the name of the publisher as given in the list should be compared with the name given on the title page of the book itself. The publisher's name is printed in the lower margin of the title page and the title page is usually the first printed page of a book.

If any titles remain unchecked after all books have been removed from the box it is evident that the books were not sent and the dealer should be notified at once. Notice should also be sent to the State Department of Education. If any book has been sent in an edition other than that specified in the list, both the dealer and Education Department should be notified so that the error may be corrected.

2. Opening the Books

Lay the book back downward on a desk or table. Press the front cover down until it touches the table, then the back cover, holding the leaves in one hand while you open a few at the back, then at the front, alternately, pressing them down gently until you reach the center of the book. This should be repeated two or three times. Never open a book violently nor bend back the covers; it is liable to break the back and to loosen the leaves. If books are opened according to the directions here given they will last much longer.

Occasionally the pages of a book require cutting. If any do it will be noticed when the book is being opened. To cut pages use a blunt paper cutter and be careful to leave a clean edge on each leaf.

3. Stamping the Books

Stamp (or write plainly and neatly) the name of the school in the upper right-hand corner of the title page and of page 17, and at the end of the last page. A rubber stamp for this purpose costs very little, and can, moreover, be used in a number of other ways in a rural school.

4. Accessioning

Enter the books in the Library Record Book according to the instructions given on the first page of that book. As soon as all books have been listed they will be ready for circulation. It does not take very long to prepare the books for circulation if the work is done according to the methods described above. No book should be given out or even used until the library has been checked up, the books opened properly and the leaves cut if necessary, and the books stamped with the library stamp and entered in the Library Record Book.

The librarian who adheres to these suggestions will find that the management of the school library is not a burden but a pleasure.

GENERAL SUGGESTIONS

Rules For Borrowers

The following rules, with such changes or additions as may seem advisable, should be copied and hung near the library case.

Borrowers—Any pupil is entitled to draw books by making application to the teacher. Any resident of the district may borrow books not needed in the school work.

Number of Volumes—Each borrower may draw one book at a time for home use.

Time Kept—A book may be kept two weeks from the date of issue and may be once renewed for the same period unless reserved for another borrower.

Fines—A fine of one cent a day shall be paid for each book kept over fourteen days without renewal. Fines will be collected for injuries to books beyond reasonable wear, for marking, turning corners of leaves, and for soiling pages or cover. No book shall be loaned to any one to whom a book or unpaid fine is charged.

Library Day

It is hoped that no school will be satisfied when it has secured one of the regular libraries but that the books will be an incentive to teachers and pupils to unite in building up a good, strong school library. To do this new books must be added regularly every year and the interest of the entire community secured. It is therefore recommended that Library Day be celebrated once a year and that the program be made so attractive that there will be a large attendance at the exercises. Such an entertainment affords an excellent opportunity for creating an interest in the reading of good books, for enlisting the support of the parents, and for securing funds for the purchase of new books.

Selection and Purchase of Additional Books

If the teacher or principal has not had any experience in selecting books for children it will be advisable for him to write to the State Department of Education for suggestions and help in selecting new books. But it is in the actual buying of books that help is most needed if books are to be secured at the lowest prices. All reputable dealers allow discounts to libraries. The amount varies on different books, but the average discount is about one-fourth. A much larger discount can usually be secured on sets and reference books. A warning should be given about buying the complete works of an author and books in series, for only the best works of an author are needed, except in the very large library, and the books in a series are usually of unequal value. "Complete libraries" which the agent recommends so highly should also be avoided.

Book agents are constantly trying to get schools to buy expensive sets of books. Such sets are ordinarily used but little and can usually be secured from a dealer for much less than the price made by the agent. A good rule to adopt is never to buy from a book agent until the worth of the book he is trying to sell has been thoroughly investigated and reliable information obtained as to the price at which the book is being sold by dealers.

APPROVED LIST OF BOOKS FOR RURAL LIBRARIES

ORIGINAL LIBRARY No. 1

The Books In This List Are Arranged Alphabetically by the Authors' Surnames

Alcott. Little Men. Little..$ 1.25
Alcott. Little Women. Little.. 1.25
Atkinson. First Studies of Plant Life. Ginn.......................... .60
Baldwin. Fairy Stories and Fables. Amer. Book Co.................. .35
Baldwin. Fifty Famous People. Amer. Book Co...................... .35
Bennett. Master Skylark. Century................................. 1.50
Benton. Saturday Mornings. Page..................................... .75
Brown. In the Days of Giants. Houghton............................ .50
Caldecott. Picture Books. v. 1-2. Warne............................ 1.00
Carpenter. Europe. Amer. Book Co................................... .70
Carpenter. How the World is Fed. (Readers on Commerce and Indus-
    try.) Amer. Book Co.. .60
Carpenter. North America. Amer. Book Co......................... .60
Carroll. Alice's Adventures in Wonderland. (Young People's Classics.)
    McKay .... .50
Champlin. Young Folks' Cyclopedia of Common Things. Holt......... 3.00
Connor and Poe. Life and Speeches of Charles Brantley Aycock.
    Mutual Pub. Co... 1.50
Defoe. Robinson Crusoe. Grosset................................... .50
Duncan. Adventures of Billy Topsail. Revell....................... 1.50
Eddy. Friends and Helpers. Ginn.................................... .60
Greene. Legends of King Arthur and His Court. Ginn............... .50
Grimm. German Household Tales. (Riverside Literature Series.)
    Houghton .... .40
Grover. Overall Boys. Rand.. .45
Harris. Uncle Remus. Appleton...................................... 2.00
Hawthorne. Wonder Book. (Riverside Literature Series.) Houghton.. .40
Hughes. Tom Brown's School-Days. Grosset.......................... .50
Husted. Stories of Indian Chieftains. Public School Pub. Co......... .40
Jackson. Nelly's Silver Mine. Little................................ 1.50
Jenks. Childhood of Ji-shib, the Ojibwa. Atkinson.................. .60
Jewett. Good Health. (Gulick Hygiene Series.) Ginn................ .40
Johnston and Barnum. Book of Plays for Little Actors. Amer. Book Co. .30
Kelly. Story of Sir Walter Raleigh. (Children's Heroes.)............ .50
Kingsley. Heroes. (Home and School Library.) Ginn............... .30
Kingsley. Water-babies. (Told to the Children.) Dutton............ .50
Kipling. Jungle Book. Century...................................... 1.50
Lamb. Tales from Shakespeare. Burt................................ .50
La Ramee. Dog of Flanders. (Bimbi Stories for Children.) Lippincott .50
Long. Ways of Wood Folk. Ginn...................................... .50
Miller. First Book of Birds. (School ed.) Houghton................ .60
Mother Goose. Book of Nursery Rhymes; arranged by Charles Welsh.
    Heath .... .30

Mulock. Little Lame Prince. (McKay's Young People's Classics.)
McKay .... $ .30
Noel. Buz. Holt........ .... 1.00
Pyle. Some Merry Adventures of Robin Hood. Scribner........ .. .50
Ruskin. King of the Golden River. (Home and School Classics.) Heath .20
Scudder. George Washington. (Riverside Literature Series.) Hough-
ton .... .40
Shaw. Big People and Little People of Other Lands (Eclectic Read-
ings.) Amer. Book Co.................... 30
Spyri. Heidi. Burt............................. .. ... 1.00
Starr. American Indians. (Ethno-geographic Reader.) Heath. .. .45
Stevenson. Treasure Island Grosset.................. 50
Stevenson. Child's Garden of Verses Rand................. ...... .50
Stone and Fickett. Everyday Life in the Colonies. Heath.......... .40
Swift. Gulliver's Travels. (Home and School Classics.) Heath..... 30
Thompson. Green Mountain Boys. Burt 1.00
Wiggin. Rebecca of Sunnybrook Farm. Grosset .... .50
Wiggin and Smith. Golden Numbers Doubleday. 2.00
Wiggin and Smith. Story Hour. Houghton............. .... 1 00
Williamson. Life of General Robert E. Lee. Johnson... .... .35

Publishers' list prices $40 40
Price to Rural Libraries 30 00

ORIGINAL LIBRARY No. 2

The Books In This List Are Arranged Alphabetically by the Authors' Surnames

Aanrud. Lisbeth Longfrock. Ginn...................................$ .40
Æsop. Child's Version of Æsop's Fables; edited by Stickney. Ginn... 35
Alcott. Little Men. Little.... .. .. 1.25
Alcott. Little Women Little........................ .... 1 25
Alderman. Classics Old and New 5v. Amer. Book Co............... 1.70
Andersen. Fairy Tales; edited by Turpin. (Graded Supplementary
Reading.) Merrill. .... .40
Arabian Nights. Stories from the Arabian Nights. (Riverside Litera-
ture Series.) Houghton........................ .. .. .40
Baker. Boys' Book of Inventions. Doubleday........ .... 2.00
Baldwin. Fairy Reader. (Eclectic Readings.) Amer. Book Co....... .35
Baldwin. Old Greek Stories (Eclectic Readings) Amer. Book Co. .. .45
Bayliss. Lolami, the Little Cliff Dweller. Public School Pub Co....... .50
Blaisdell and Ball. Hero Stories from American History. Ginn.. ..... .50
Bradish. Old Norse Stories. (Eclectic Readings.) Amer. Book Co.... .45
Brown. Plant Baby and Its Friends. Silver...................... .48
Bunyan. Pilgrim's Progres. (Riverside School Library.) Houghton... .60
Carpenter. Africa Amer. Book Co. .... .60
Carpenter. North America. Amer. Book Co....... 60
Carroll. Alice's Adventures in Wonderland. McKay.................. .50
Connor. Makers of North Carolina History. Thompson 65
Cooper. Last of the Mohicans. Grosset........ 50
Cumnock. School Speaker. McClurg.......... 75

Dodge. Hans Brinker. Grosset...................................$ .50
Eggleston. Stories of Great Americans. (Eclectic Readings.) Amer.
    Book Co.. .40
Francillon. Gods and Heroes. (Home and School Library.) Ginn..... .40
Fultz. The Flyaways and Other Seed Travelers. Public School Pub. Co. .60
Grover. Sunbonnet Babies' Primer. Rand.......................... .40
Guerber. Story of the Thirteen Colonies. (Eclectic Readings.) Amer.
    Book Co. .... .65
Hawthorne. Wonder Book. (Riverside Literature Series.) Houghton .40
Husted. Stories of Indian Children. Public School Pub. Co.......... .50
Jewett. Betty Leicester. Houghton................................ 1.25
Johnston and Chapin. Home Occupations for Boys and Girls. Jacobs. .50
Keller. Story of My Life. Grosset................................. .50
Lang. Blue Fairy Book. Burt...................................... 1.00
Lyman. Story Telling. McClurg.................................... 1.00
Montgomery. Anne of Green Gables. Grosset........................ .50
Morley. Bee People. McClurg...................................... .50
Mother Goose. Book of Nursery Rhymes, arranged by Charles Welsh,
    Heath .... .30
Mulock. Adventures of a Brownie. Ed. Pub. Co..................... .40
Mulock. John Halifax, Gentleman. Crowell......................... .60
O'Shea. Six Nursery Classics. (Home and School Classics.) Heath.. .30
Pier. Harding of St. Timothy's. Houghton......................... 1.50
Porter. Pollyanna. Page.. 1.25
Potter. Tale of Benjamin Bunny. Warne........................... .50
Robbins. High School Debate Book. McClurg........................ 1.00
Roberts. Kindred of the Wild. Grosset............................ .75
Ruskin. King of the Golden River. (Home and School Classics.) Heath .20
Sargent. Corn Plants. Houghton.................................. .75
Sewell. Black Beauty. Crowell.................................... .60
Starr. Strange Peoples. Heath.................................... .40
Stevenson. Days and Deeds; a Book of Verse. Doubleday............ 1.25
Stevenson. Treasure Island. Grosset.............................. .50
Stoddard. Red Mustang. Harper................................... .60
Tappan. European Hero Stories. Houghton......................... .65
Trowbridge. Tinkham Brothers' Tide-Mill. Lothrop................. 1.25
Wiggin. Birds' Christmas Carol. Houghton......................... .50
Wiggin. Polly Oliver's Problem. (Riverside Literature Series.) Hough-
    ton .... .40
Wyss. Swiss Family Robinson. Grosset............................ .50
Zollinger. Widow O'Callaghan's Boys. McClurg..................... 1.25

    Publishers' List Prices..................................:..$39.73
    Price to Rural Libraies 30.00

SUPPLEMENTAL LIBRARY No. 1

The Books In This List Are Arranged Alphabetically by the Authors' Surnames

Alcott. Jo's Boys. Little..$ 1.25
Beard. American Boys' Handy Book. Scribner...................... 2.00
Bryant. Stories to Tell to Children. Houghton..................... 1.00

Carroll. Through the Looking Glass. Macmillan....................$ .50
Cox. Palmer Cox Brownie Primer. Century......................... .50
Chamberlain. How We Are Sheltered. (Home and World Series.)
    Macmillan .... .40
Champlin. Young Folks' Cyclopedia of Persons and Places. Holt...... 3.00
Dickens. Christmas Carol and the Cricket on the Hearth. (Pocket
    Classics.) Macmillan... .25
Dix. Merrylips. Macmillan....................................... .75
Eggleston. Stories of American Life and Adventure. (Eclectic Read-
    ings). Amer. Book Co. .... .50
Ewing. Jackanapes. (Home and School Classics.) Page............ .50
Gibson. Blossom Hosts and Insect Guests. Newson.................. .80
Goodrich. First Book of Farming. Doubleday..................... 1.00
Hawthorne. Tanglewood Tales. (Riverside Literature Series.) Houghton .40
Inman. Ranch on the Oxhide. Macmillan.......................... .50
Kelman. Stories from the Life of Christ. (Told to the Children
    Series.) Dutton.. .50
Morley. Seed Babies. Ginn...................................... .25
Porter. Laddie. Doubleday...................................... 1.35
Robbins. High School Debate Book. McClurg...................... 1.00
Sage and Cooley. Occupations for Little Fingers. Scribner.......... 1.00
Scudder. Book of Fables and Folk Stories. Houghton.............. .45
Segur. Story of a Donkey, abridged by Charles Welsh. Heath........ .20
Seton. Rolf in the Woods. Grosset.............................. .50
Tappan. American Hero Stories. Houghton........................ .55
Wiltse. Folklore Stories and Proverbs. Ginn..................... .30

    Publishers' List Prices..$20.05
    Price to Rural Libraries....................................... 15.00

SUPPLEMENTAL LIBRARY No. 2

The Books in This List Are Arranged Alphabetically by the Authors' Surnames

Alcott. Old-fashioned Girl. Little..................................$1.25
Bacon. Songs Every Child Should Know. Doubleday................. .90
Blanchan. Birds That Every Child Should Know. Doubleday.......... .50
Brooks. Stories of the Red Children. Ed. Pub. Co. .... .40
Carpenter. South America. Amer. Book Co. .... .60
Chamberlain. How We Are Fed. Macmillan........................ .40
Champlin. Young Folks' Cyclopedia of Persons and Places. Holt..... 3.00
Collodi. Pinocchio; translated from the Italian by W. S. Cramp. Ginn. .40
Connor and Poe. Life and Speeches of Charles Brantley Aycock. Mutual
    Pub. Co. 1.50
Cox. Palmer Cox Brownie Primer. Century....................... .40
Finnemore. Japan. (Peeps at Many Lands.) Black................. .75
Greene. Pickett's Gap. (Standard School Library). Macmillan...... .50
Jacobs. English Fairy Tales. Burt............................... .50
Kelly. Short Stories of Our Shy Neighbors. (Eclectic School Read-
    ings.) Amer. Book Co. .... .50

Lane and Hill. American History in Literature. Ginn..............$ .50
Long. Secrets of the Woods. Ginn................................... .50
McDonald and Dalrymple. Kathleen in Ireland. Little............... .60
Morgan. How to Dress a Doll. Altemus............................ .50
Munroe. Flamingo Feather. Harper............................... .60
Poe. A Southerner in Europe. Mutual Pub. Co. .... .75
Repplier. Book of Famous Verse. (Riverside Library for Young
    People.) Houghton.. .75
Richards. Florence Nightingale. Appleton......................... 1.25
Seawell. Little Jarvis. (Young Heroes of Our Navy.) Appleton...... 1.00
Stack. Wild Flowers Every Child Should Know. Doubleday.......... .50
Stoddard. Two Arrows. Harper................................... .60

    Publishers' List Prices.......................................$19.15
    Price to Rural Libraries...................................... 15.00

SUPPLEMENTAL LIBRARY No. 3

The Books In This List Are Arranged Alphabetically by the Authors' Surnames

Aanrud. Lisbeth Longfrock. Ginn................................ $ .40
Andersen. Fairy Tales; edited by Turpin. (Graded Supplementary
    Reading.) Merrill .... .40
Bryant. How to Tell Stories to Children. Houghton................ 1.00
Carpenter. North America. Amer. Book Co. .... .60
Champlin. Young Folks' Cyclopedia of Common Things. Holt........ 3.00
Connor. Makers of North Carolina History. Thompson.............. .65
Connor and Poe. Life and Speeches of Charles Brantley Aycock. Mutual
    Pub. Co. 1.50
Cumnock. School Speaker. McClurg.............................. .75
Johnston and Barnum. Book of Plays for Little Actors. Amer. Book Co. .30
Kelly. Story of Sir Walter Raleigh. (Children's Heroes.) Dutton.... .50
Montgomery. Anne of Green Gables. Grosset...................... .50
Noel. Buz. Holt... 1.00
Norton. Heart of Oak Books. 7 v. Heath......................... 3.10
Porter. Pollyanna. Page....................................... 1.25
Potter. Tale of Benjamin Bunny. Warne......................... .50
Pyle. Some Merry Adventures of Robin Hood. Scribner............. .50
Sargent. Corn Plants. Houghton................................ .75
Spyri. Heidi. Burt 1.00
Stoddard. Red Mustang. Harper................................. .60
Stone and Fickett. Everyday Life in the Colonies. Heath............ .40
Trowbridge. Tinkham Brothers' Tide Mill. Lothrop................. 1.25
Wiggin. Rebecca of Sunnybrook Farm. Grosset.................... .50

    Publishers' List Prices.......................................$20.45
    Price to Rural Libraries...................................... 15.00

ORIGINAL LIBRARY No. 1

Books Classified According to Subject

STORIES

Alcott, L. M. Little Women

This story of the happy home life of four girls, Meg, Jo, Beth, and Amy, is drawn largely from the girlhood life of Miss Alcott and her sisters. It is so good and wholesome in every way and so universally popular that it has been pronounced the best of all stories for girls.

Alcott, L. M. Little Men

A sequel to Little Women and almost as good. Tells of the doings of Jo's boys and girls at Plumfield.

Bennett, John. Master Skylark

The story of a lovable little lad who lived at the same time as Shakespeare. He goes to London, meets the great Shakespeare himself, and has many interesting adventures. The book is well written and cannot fail to arouse interst in Shakespearean literature. And it is also an excellent story.

Caldecott, Randolph. Picture Books. 2 volumes

Volume one contains the Diverting History of John Gilpin, the Three Jovial Huntsmen, and an Elegy on the Death of a Mad Dog. Volume two contains the House that Jack Built, Sing a Song of Six-pence, and the Queen of Hearts.

These are miniature and cheaper editions of the books by this famous illustrator, but they are dainty little volumes with beautiful pictures in color and in black and white.

Defoe, Daniel. Robinson Crusoe

Why write a note about this well known classic which is one of the greatest tales of adventure and of shipwreck ever written? If it is necessary to create an interest in this story read aloud the account (beginning on page 233 of how Crusoe found his man Friday and how he taught him to speak English.

Duncan, Norman. Adventures of Billy Topsail

These stories are based upon real incidents in the lives of Billy Topsail and his friends—Labrador boys who are merry and brave, kind and self-reliant. This is a book for the oldest boys in the school and one which the fathers and older brothers may also read and enjoy.

Grover, E. O. Overall Boys; a First Reader

This reader is remarkable in several ways. The paper, print and binding are excellent; the illustrations are so good and so attractive that it gives even a grown person real pleasure to run through it; and, unlike most readers, it consists of one long story and not numerous short ones.

Hughes, Thomas. Tom Brown's School Days

. This story of school life under the famous Dr. Rugby is probably the best school story ever written. The teacher should remember, however, that it depicts English school life and that many American boys and girls will find it tedious at first. Read a "starter" in class, for it is a pity for any boy or girl to miss this book. The reading aloud of chapter five, "Rugby and Football," never fails to awaken interest and to make the book intensely popular. This is another volume for the grown folks as well as the older boys and girls.

Jackson, H. H. Nelly's Silver Mine

How Nelly and Rob March moved from New England to Colorado in the early seventies and how Nelly discovered a silver mine. It is so difficult to find really good wholesome stories for girls that this exceptionally fine one should be in every school library.

La Ramee, Louise de. The Dog of Flanders

An appealing tale of the devotion and faithfulness of a big dog and of the kindness and affection of his little master. A bit sad but a Christmas story well adapted for reading aloud.

Spyri, Johanna. Heidi

Heidi and her old grandfather lived in a hut in the Swiss Alps. She had many exciting experiences with Peter, a herd boy, and with a little girl from the city. The story is charmingly written and is one of the best for children in the intermediate grades. Good for reading aloud.

Stevenson, R. L. Treasure Island

An exciting tale of hidden treasures and pirates written especially for boys but it will be enjoyed by everyone who loves a story of pure adventure. Stevenson himself wrote of this book: "It's all about a map and a treasure, and a mutiny and a derelict ship, and a current, and a fine old Squire Trelawney, and a doctor, and another doctor, and a seacock with one leg, and a sea-song with the chorus 'Yo-ho-ho and a bottle of rum.'"

Swift, Jonathan. Gulliver's Travels

Mr. Lemuel Gulliver tells of his shipwreck at sea, his strange adventures among the Lilliputians and his dangerous encounters with the giants of Brobdingnag. For older boys.

Thompson, D. P. Green Mountain Boys

Tells how Fort Ticonderoga was captured and other exploits of Ethan Allen and the "Green Mountain Boys." Special attention should be called to the book when a class is studying this period of United States history.

Wiggin, Mrs. K. D. Rebecca of Sunnybrook Farm

Rebecca Rowena Randall goes from Sunnybrook Farm to live with her Aunt Mirandy, a hard stern woman, who is to help her to an education which is to be the "making of her." The aunt fails to understand the fearless, honest, impulsive, beauty-loving child. The things which Rebecca does are enough to astonish less conservative people than Miss Miranda; but it would take a heart even harder than hers to steel itself against the child's charm. A fine wholesome story which big sister and mother will also enjoy.

MYTHS, FAIRY STORIES, AND FABLES

Baldwin, James. Fairy Stories and Fables

An excellent collection. Includes such favorites as the Three Bears, Little Red Riding Hood, Tom Thumb, Jack and the Beanstalk, and Cinderella.

Brown, A. F. In the days of Giants

Stories of giants, and the most readable and attractive collection of Norse myths for children.

Carroll, Lewis. Alice's Adventures in Wonderland

The best of all nonsense books and one that has become a classic. It is a new kind of fairy tale which children love because of its absurd distortion of familiar facts and grown people because of its quaint humor and comic undermeanings. A school library without a copy of this book is like a room without light and sunshine.

Greene, F. N. Legends of King Arthur and His Court

Simple versions in prose of some of Tennyson's Idylls of the King. Useful to the story-teller and well adapted for reading aloud.

Grimm, J. L. & W. K. German Household Tales

The Grimm Brothers collected the folk stories of the Germans and charmingly retold them for children. Various collections and editions of the Grimm fairy tales have been issued but the one listed above contains an unusually wise choice of the stories.

In the Grimm fairy tales "the princes and princesses are childlike men and women; they are good and therefore beautiful. They do right . . . and live happily. All folk tales follow this common law, which is at its best in the old tales of Grimm."

Harris, J. C. Uncle Remus; his Songs and Sayings

In spite of its poor wearing qualities and price this book is included in a $30 library, for every child should know and love the Uncle Remus tales. The illustrations by Mr. Frost are delightful.

Hawthorne, Nathaniel. Wonder Book for Girls and Boys

The best version of the Greek myths for children who have a large vocabulary and read easily but for the younger children Baldwin's Old Greek Stories (see Library No. 2) is better. This edition of the Wonder Book has attractive illustrations, notes, index of mythology, and a list of poems and stories for supplementary reading.

Kingsley, Charles. Heroes; or, Greek Fairy Tales for my Children

Stories of Perseus, Jason and Theseus which emphasize courage and bravery and inspire hero worship.

Kingsley, Charles. Water-babies

The story of the little chimney sweep who was turned into a water baby is given here just as Kingsley told it but the long words and puzzling references to philosophical and scientific problems are left out. It is an excellent adaptation and the beautiful colored illustrations add much to the attractiveness of the little book.

Mother Goose. Book of Nursery Rhymes, arranged by Charles Welsh

Every home and every school should have some kind of a collection of Mother Goose melodies. The edition listed here is the best cheap edition while the collection edited by Wheeler is carefully selected and well illustrated and is probably the best for the school library which can afford a more expensive edition ($1.50).

Mulock, D. M. Little Lame Prince

A modern fairy tale which teaches patience and other virtues and points a good many morals, but it is most delightful reading nevertheless.

Pyle, Howard. Some Merry Adventures of Robin Hood

Excellent abridgment of the author's larger and more expensive book ($3.00).

This is the book to give to boys who love adventure, for it tells "how in merry England, in the times of old, there lived within the green glades of Sherwood Forest a famous outlaw whose name was Robin Hood and how he was attended by seven score yoeman bold who helped him in his mad adventures."

Ruskin, John. King of the Golden River

The King of the Golden River has been pronounced the most beautiful sermon ever preached to children in the guise of a fairy tale.

NATURE AND SCIENCE

Atkinson, G. F. First Studies of Plant Life

It is not easy to get a good elementary book on this subject but this is one of the best and one of the most popular. Well adapted for class-room use.

Eddy, S. J. Friends and Helpers

Well selected stories and verses about animals, birds and insects. The illustrations are appropriate and very attractive.

Kipling, Rudyard. Jungle Book

Stories of animal life in the jungle.

Long, W. J. Ways of Wood Folk

Stories which not only inspire enthusiasm and love for animals, but teach habits of observation. Foxes, rabbits, bears and birds are Mr. Long's familiar friends and his stories make you wish they were also yours.

Miller, Mrs. O. T. First Book of Birds

All about the daily life of the bird, his habits, and his education; how he travels, sleeps, and changes his clothes; how he is made and how he works for us.

A book of this class for children should be clear, simple, accurate, and well illustrated; Mrs. Miller's book is exceptionally good in these respects, and, although not written in story form, is yet very interesting.

Colored illustrations of the most common birds, and black and white illustrations of the others add greatly to the attractiveness and value of the book.

Noel, Maurice. Buz; the Life of a Honey Bee

A lively story depicting the life and adventures of a honey bee. It is good considered purely as a story and also has some value as natural history.

HOME ECONOMICS AND HYGIENE

Benton, C. F. Saturday Mornings

What Christmas brought a little girl and how she learned housekeeping on Saturday mornings. The book is practical and valuable although it presupposes better equipment in some instances than many homes possess.

Carpenter, F. G. How the World is Fed

The author explains in the preface that the purpose of the book is to give the children a knowledge of the production and preparation of foods and to show how civilization and commerce grew from man's need of food and the exchange of foods between the different nations of the earth.

The author takes the children on personally conducted tours and to-
gether they visit the great wheat fields and follow the grain to the
mills and from the mills to the markets; they go through the corn belts
and the rice countries; and to a western cattle ranch and follow the
cattle to the stock yards. Visits are paid to dairy countries, to the poul-
try yards of the world, to the great fishing grounds and to many other
centers of commerce and industry.

An excellent supplementary reader.

Jewett, F. G. Good Health

A readable and sensible little book dealing with the care of the body
and personal habits.

BIOGRAPHY, DESCRIPTION, AND HISTORY

Baldwin, James. Fifty Famous People

Stories of Lincoln, King Alfred, Cyrus the Great, Robert Bruce, and
many other famous people.

Connor and Poe. Life and Speeches of Charles Brantley Aycock

Life of North Carolina's educational Governor and a collection of some
of his best speeches.

Kelly, M. D. Story of Sir Walter Raleigh

Sir Walter Raleigh is one of the favorite heroes of children, especially
of North Carolina children, and no wonder, for the story of his life is as
wonderful as any fairy tale. Hence this attractive little volume with
colored illustrations will be very popular.

Scudder, H. E. George Washington

One of the best lives of Washington for young readers, and probably
the best brief biography for readers of any age.

Williamson, Mrs. M. L. Life of General Robert E. Lee

A life of Lee for children.

Carpenter, F. G. Europe

"It is the children themselves . . . who climb the Alps and stand
on the North Cape watching the sun shine at midnight, . . . go from
city to city, from farm to farm, and factory to factory, seeing how the
various peoples live and what they are doing in the work of the world.
It is they who are admitted to the palaces, parliaments, and public of-
fices where they learn how each nation is governed and something as to
its civilization, commerce and trade."

Carpenter, F. G. North America

The children, traveling through the United States, British America,
Mexico and Central America, go through the cotton and tobacco plantations of the South, visit the orange groves of Florida, go down into
the mines, visit lumber camps and hunt for game. Mr. Carpenter knows
how to write for children and his geographical readers are popular with
young people and indispensable for supplementary reading.

Shaw, E. R. Big People and Little People of Other Lands

Another good supplementary reader which tells about the big and
little people of many lands.

Stone and Fickett. Everyday Life in the Colonies

Stories of early customs and celebrations. Useful for supplementary
reading with the United States history classes.

Husted, M. H. Stories of Indian Chieftains

These stories vividly portray the conflict between the Indian and the white man from the discovery of America to our own times.

Jenks, A. E. Childhood of Ji-shib, the Ojibwa

Books about Indians are always in demand and this is one of the best. It appeals to the child, especially the boy, because the author so clearly and sympathetically reveals the real life and soul of the Indian boy.

Starr, Frederick. American Indians

About the dress, weapons, games and ceremonials of the various tribes of American Indians.

POETRY AND PLAYS

Stevenson, R. L. Child's Garden of Verses

The simple rhythm of these poems appeals to children. This is a very attractive edition illustrated in color.

Wiggin and Smith. Golden Numbers

This is considered the best poetry collection for children. The poems are classified acording to subject and prefacing each division is a page of comment on, and appreciation of, the poems that follow.

Johnston and Barnum. Book of Plays for Little Actors

Very simple little plays for reading or acting in the primary grades. Some of the plays are drawn from nursery classics and some are designed for the celebration of special days.

Lamb, Charles and Lamb, Mary. Tales from Shakespeare

These tales, founded on twenty of Shakespeare's plays, have taken their place as a children's classic.

BOOKS FOR REFERENCE USE

Champlin, J. D. Young Folks Cyclopedia of Common Things

This little cyclopedia, covering natural science and useful arts, contains brief simple articles that children can understand. It is also a valuable book for teaching the use of an encyclopedia, and hence it has a two-fold value in the rural school library.

Wiggin and Smith. Story Hour

Stories for reading aloud or for telling which may be used even in the lowest grades. What makes the book especially useful to the busy teacher or mother is that the stories do not require any adaptation or arrangement but can be used just as they are given. The introduction on story-telling in the school room is delightful and contains many good suggestions for the inexperienced story-teller.

ORIGINAL LIBRARY No. 2

Books Classified According to Subject

STORIES

Aanrud, Hans. Lisbeth Longfrock

Charming story of life on a farm in Norway and of little Lisbeth Longfrock who reaches the height of her ambition when she becomes head milkmaid on the Hoel farm.

Alcott, L. M. Little Women

This story of the happy home life of four girls, Meg, Jo, Beth, and Amy, is drawn largely from the girlhood life of Miss Alcott and her sisters. It is so good and wholesome in every way and so universally popular that it has been pronounced the best of all stories for girls.

Alcott, L. M. Little Men

A sequel to Little Women and almost as good. Tells of the doings of Jo's boys and girls at Plumfield.

Bunyan, John. Pilgrim's Progress

Pilgrim's Progress, one of the great books of the world, was written in prison by John Bunyan who died in London over two hundred years ago. Many children will not read it for themselves but few of them will fail to be interested if it is to read them.

Cooper, J. F. Last of the Mohicans

There are few boys who will not read Cooper. They like the adventure and they like the fighting. The last of the Mohicans is the second of the Leatherstocking tales and is a story of Fort William Henry during the French and Indian war.

Defoe, Daniel. Robinson Crusoe

Why write a note about this well known classic which is one of the greatest tales of adventure and of shipwreck ever written? If it is necessary to create an interest in this story read aloud the account (beginning on page 233) of how Crusoe found his man Friday and how he taught him to speak English.

Dodge, Mrs. M. M. Hans Brinker

A story of Hans and Gretel, of the courage of the Dutch people, and of a skating journey from Amsterdam to The Hague.

Grover, E. O. Sunbonnet Babies' Primer

An excellent primer, delightfully illustrated, and a real joy to little children even before they have learned to read.

Jewett, S. O. Betty Leicester

Betty, who had always lived abroad, returns when she is fifteen and spends the summer in a New England country town. A good wholesome story.

Montgomery, L. M. Anne of Green Gables

Anne is a lively, imaginative child from a Nova Scotia asylum who is adopted by an elderly farmer and his sister. A good school story, interesting to young girls and to most adults.

Mulock, D. M. John Halifax, Gentleman

When the older girls and boys demand a love story give them John Halifax, for there is nothing purer and sweeter. It is the life story of a man whose courage and faithfulness to high ideals win him the right to be called by "the grand old name of Gentleman."

Pier, A. S. Harding of St. Timothy's

An excellent boarding school story for boys, wholesome in spirit and thoroughly manly in tone.

Porter, E. H. Pollyanna

Pollyanna, after the death of her father, a western missionary, goes to live with her aunt in Vermont. She takes with her the "glad game" which she had learned from her father, and not only plays it herself, but persuades a great many others to play it with her. So Miss Polly's niece works a wonderful transformation in the community. Pollyanna is a book to read to old people, to sick people, and to young people, and whoever reads it or hears it read will be very likely to try to play the "glad game" too.

Potter, Beatrix. Tale of Benjamin Bunny

A delightfully illustrated book which will be very popular with the little children. It tells how Peter Rabbit lost his clothes and how Benjamin Bunny helped to find them.

Sewell, Anna. Black Beauty

Black Beauty is a horse and he himself tells the story of his life. This is considered the best book published to cultivate a spirit of kindness for horses.

Stevenson, R. L. Treasure Island

An exciting tale of hidden treasures and pirates written especially for boys but it will be enjoyed by everyone who loves a story of pure adventure. Stevenson himself wrote of this book: "It's all about a map and a treasure, and a mutiny and a derelict ship, and a current, and a fine old Squire Trelawney, and a doctor, and another doctor, and a seacock with one leg, and a sea-song with the chorus 'Yo-ho-ho and a bottle of rum.' "

Stoddard, W. O. Red Mustang

A story of the Mexican border, telling how Cal Evans was captured by a band of Indians, and how Dick, the Red Mustang, saved his life.

Trowbridge, J. T. Tinkham Brothers' Tide Mill

"The successful fight of a family of boys to defend their rights and earn an honest living for their widowed mother, their sister and themselves. Mr. Trowbridge may not be a great writer, but he goes directly to the boyish heart."

Wiggin, Mrs. K. D. Birds' Christmas Carol

How Sarah Maud, Peoria, Cornelius, Baby Larry and the rest of the nine little Ruggleses went to a Christmas dinner party given by Carol Bird, a little invalid, who was born on Christmas day.

This story makes a good play for a school entertainment and the Library Commission will be glad to lend a dramatized version without charge to any teacher applying for it.

Wiggin, Mrs. K. D. Polly Oliver's Problem

A good wholesome story for girls. Polly is a bright, attractive girl and her problem is how to earn her living.

Wyss, J. D. Swiss Family Robinson

Stories of shipwreck and of strange adventures always appeal to boys and this is one of the best ever written. The Robinson family "did sail in the tubs, and train zebras and ostriches for riding, and grow apples and pines in the same garden; and why shouldn't they?"

Zollinger, Gulielma. Widow O'Callaghan's Boys

Story of how Mrs. O'Callaghan and her seven sons earn a living and an account of the sensible way in which one mother brought up her boys.

MYTHS, FAIRY STORIES, AND FABLES

Aesop. Child's Version of Aesop's Fables

This volume contains the best fables arranged as a supplementary reader for children eight or nine years of age. There are 125 fables by Aesop, the slave of Samos, and 31 by La Fontaine and Krilof.

Andersen, H. C. Fairy Tales, edited by Turpin

A good collection for the younger children intended as a supplementary reader. The beautiful fairy tales of Andersen, although modern, have the true folklore spirit.

Arabian Nights. Stories from the Arabian Nights

Children should be familiar with the best of the Arabian Nights stories in order to understand the meaning of such common expressions as "Aladdin's Lamp," "Sinbad's Jewels," and "Open sesame." But teachers and parents should remember that many editions of the Arabian Nights are unfit for children. The stories contained in the volume listed here have been wisely selected and carefully edited.

Baldwin, James. Fairy Reader

Very simple adaptations of tales from Grimm and Andersen for youngest readers. The book is designed to be used as a supplementary reader and each story is preceded by a list of the more difficult words.

Baldwin, James. Old Greek Stories

The best edition of the Greek myths for the fourth and fifth grades. The stories are told, not as stories of gods, but as hero stories. For the older boys and girls Hawthorne's Wonder Book (see below) is recommended.

Bradish, S. P. Old Norse Stories

A good collection of Norse myths for the younger children.

Carroll, Lewis. Alice's Adventures in Wonderland

The best of all nonsense books and one that has become a classic. It is a new kind of fairy tale which children love because of its absurd distortion of familiar facts and grown people because of its quaint humor and comic undermeanings. A school library without a copy of this book is like a room without light and sunshine.

Francillon, R. E. Gods and Heroes

The author ignores the difference between the gods of Greece and the gods of Rome and covers the whole field of mythology in one continuous story. This little volume is very different from Hawthorne's "Wonder Book" and Kingsley's "Heroes," and is better for the younger children.

Hawthorne, Nathaniel. Wonderbook

The best version of the Greek myths for children who have a large vocabulary and read easily but for the younger children Baldwin's Old Greek Stories (see above) is better. This edition of the Wonder Book has attractive illustrations, notes, an index of mythology, and a list of poems and stories for supplementary reading.

Lang, Andrew. Blue Fairy Book

A good collection of the best known fairy tales including such favorites as Little Red Riding Hood, Sleeping Beauty and Pretty Goldilocks.

Lang has compiled a number of books of fairy tales, the best being the "Yellow Fairy Book," the Red and the Green. The Grey and the Crimson are unfit for children's reading.

Mother Goose. Book of Nursery Rhymes, arranged by Charles Welsh

Every home and every school should have some kind of a collection of Mother Goose melodies. The edition listed here is the best cheap edition while the collection edited by Wheeler is carefully selected and well illustrated and is probably the best for the school library which can afford a more expensive edition ($1.50).

Mulock, D. M. Adventures of a Brownie

An old time fairy tale in which a house brownie plays all kinds of tricks on some children, but only on the cross and disagreeable ones.

O'Shea, M. V. Six Nursery Classics

A well arranged and attractively illustrated little book for the youngest children. Contains The House that Jack Built, Mother Hubbard, Cock Robin, Dame Wiggins, Old Woman and Her Pig, and The Three Bears.

Ruskin, John. King of the Golden River

The King of the Golden River has been pronounced the most beautiful sermon ever preached to children in the guise of a fairy tale.

NATURE AND SCIENCE

Bayliss, C. K. Lolami, the Little Cliff Dweller

"Portrays carefully the cliff-dweller's life and surroundings, in the story of a little boy's adventures before the coming of the white man."

Brown, K. L. Plant Baby and Its Friends

A nature reader for primary grades, well written and accurate, but it should be used for class room reading.

Fultz, F. M. The Flyaways and Other Seed Travelers

Very interesting stories about seeds which children may read for themselves. Teachers will find it useful in language work and story-telling.

Morley, M. W. Bee People

This is considered one of the most successful nature books ever written for children. The book is well illustrated and very attractive in appearance.

Roberts, C. G. D. Kindred of the Wild

An excellent collection of animal stories for the older boys and for their fathers and big brothers.

USEFUL ARTS

Baker, R. S. Boys' Book of Inventions

Stories of the wonders of modern science which are really interesting and very popular with boys.

Johnston and Chapin. Home Occupations for Boys and Girls

A book for mothers and teachers to use with little children. Only very simple materials are required.

Sargent, F. L. Corn Plants

Presents in an attractive way information regarding six of the most important plants in the world—wheat, oats, rye, barley, rice and maize. The book is intended as a supplementary reader and it can also be used to advantage in the preparation of teachers' talks.

BIOGRAPHY, DESCRIPTION, AND HISTORY

Blaisdell and Ball. Hero Stories from American History

This book is intended to be used as a supplementary historical reader in the sixth and seventh grades. It includes the most notable and dramatic events of the first fifty years of our national life—stories of Nathan Hale, George Rogers Clark, Washington, Anthony Wayne, Andrew Jackson, etc.

Eggleston, Edward. Stories of Great Americans for Little Americans

"It is one of the purposes of these stories," says the author in the preface, "to make the mind of the pupil familiar with some of the leading figures in the history of our country by means of personal anecdote."

Guerber, H. A. Story of the Thirteen Colonies

Another good historical reader. Includes events and anecdotes dealing with United States history from the discovery to the close of the Revolution.

Husted, M. H. Stories of Indian Children

Pictures the life of the Indian before the coming of the white man.

Tappan, E. M. European Hero Stories

The main object of the book is to give the child some background for the study of American history.

Connor, R. D. W. Makers of North Carolina History

This book emphasizes the personalities of the great leaders of North Carolina rather than the events in which they were concerned.

Keller, Helen. Story of My Life

Life and letters of this remarkable woman, blind and deaf from infancy. It is an inspiring story of marvelous achievements for the older boys and girls and for men and women.

Carpenter, F. G. Africa

Describes the country, the peoples, the animals, and the industries of the Africa of today. Similar to his other geographical readers.

Carpenter, F. G. North America

The children, traveling through the United States, British America, Mexico, and Central America, go through the cotton and tobacco plantations of the South, visit the orange groves of Florida, go down into the mines, visit lumber camps, and hunt for game. Mr. Carpenter knows how to write for children, and his geographical readers are popular with young people and indispensable for supplementary reading.

Starr, Frederick. Strange Peoples

One of the few good geographical readers. Describes the strange people of North and South America, Europe, Asia, Africa and the Philippines.

COLLECTIONS OF LITERATURE

Alderman, E. A. Classics Old and New. Five volumes

These readers are included in this library because except for the first 38 pages of Volume 1, all of the stories are recognized classics. Contain good material for the Friday afternoon exercises.

Cumnock, R. M. School Speaker

An excellent collection of recitations and speeches for the grades.

Lyman, Edna. Story Telling; What to Tell and How to Tell It

A valuable book for teachers and parents, containing especially good material for story-telling to older children.

Robbins, E. C. High School Debate Book

The best elementary book on debating. Gives valuable suggestions on how to debate, a model constitution and by-laws for a literary society, and briefs and refernces on 18 important political and social questions of the day.

Stevenson, B. E. Days and Deeds; a book of verse

A collection of poetry for children's reading and speaking. The selections are grouped under holidays, special days, names of great Americans, poetry of the seasons and a few of the best lyrics. It is especially useful in preparing programs for the observance of Christmas or Thanksgiving, Hallowe'en or St. Valentine's day, Bird day, or Arbor day, etc. It also contains some of the best verse that has been written about 67 famous Americans, including such names as Longfellow, Louisa May Alcott, Andrew Jackson, Robert E. Lee, and Frances Willard.

SUPPLEMENTAL LIBRARY No. 1

Books Classified According to Subject

STORIES

Alcott, L. M. Jo's Boys

Sequel to Little Men, telling how Aunt Jo's Little Men and Little Women turned out.

Cox, Palmer. Palmer Cox Brownie Primer

There are no more attractive picture books than the Brownie books of which there are six. But these books are expensive ($1.50 each) and do not wear very well. The Palmer Cox Brownie Primer is an excellent substitute and is always popular with the little children. Brownies swarm on every page intent on mischief and merrymaking, and stories, mostly in rhyme, accompany the pictures, but the illustrations are the important part.

Dickens, Charles. Christmas Carol and the Cricket on the Hearth

The Christman Carol, a ghost story of Christmas, is a masterpiece of English literature. This short story contains the whole gospel of Christmas and it "made a whole generation keep Christmas with acts of helpfulness to the poor." The Cricket on the Hearth, a fairy tale of home, is also a Christmas story and it gives us an ideal picture of neighborly kindness and family affection.

These are good stories with which to introduce young people to Dickens. The Christmas Carol is excellent for reading aloud and the Cricket on the Hearth has often been produced on the stage.

Dix, B. M. Merrylips

An unusually fine story, interesting, wholesome and accurate historically. It is a story of Roundheads and Cavaliers and of a little girl who wanted to be a boy.

Ewing, J. H. Jackanapes

A Damon and Pythias story. An English boy, mischievous but truehearted, dies in battle to save the life of a friend. The pathos appeals to girls and the nobility and bravery of the young hero to boys.

Inman, Henry. Ranch on the Oxhide

A story of boys' and girls' life on the frontier. It is a story of wolves and panthers, and buffaloes and Indians, and of Buffalo Bill and General Custer. No better book can be found for the boy who craves the Jesse James type of story.

Porter, Mrs. G. S. Laddie

The books of Mrs. Gene Stratton Porter really have no place in a list of this kind, but Laddie is included because it gives such a good, attractive picture of country life. The story is told by the "Little Sister," who, with her mother and father, and brothers and sisters, lives on a farm in Indiana. Her love of nature, her devotion to Laddie, the oldest brother, the mystery in the family, and Laddie's love affair are the chief features of this country-life story.

Segur, S. R. Story of a Donkey

A good animal story told by Neddy, the donkey. It is a short story well adapted for reading aloud.

Seton, E. T. Rolf in the Woods

Rolf, a fifteen-year-old boy, runs away from his uncle and lives with an Indian for several years in the woods. He learns much forest lore which in the war of 1812 makes him valuable as a scout. Although the story is long, it is interesting to boys, especially to boy scouts.

MYTHS, FAIRY STORIES, AND FABLES

Carroll, Lewis. Through the Looking Glass

Continuation of Alice in Wonderland and just as good. Contains the famous poem, "The Walrus and the Carpenter."

Hawthorne, Nathaniel. Tanglewood Tales

A second Wonder-book. See note on Wonder-book, page 16.

Scudder, H. E. Book of Fables

A good collection of fables, chiefly from Aesop. The preface contains an excellent argument for the use of such literature with little children.

Wiltse, S. E. Folklore Stories and Proverbs

A good collection for children who are just learning to read.

NATURE AND SCIENCE

Gibson, W. H. Blossom Hosts and Insect Guests

A most interesting study of flower fertilization which tells how the flowers welcome the bee, fly, wasp and other insects. The book is illustrated by the author.

Morley, M. W. Seed Babies

About beans, peas, nuts, etc., which talk to a little boy and tell him how they grow.

USEFUL ARTS

Beard, D. C. What to Do and How to Do It; the American Boy's Handy Book

Directions for making kites, boats, fishing tackle, magic lanterns, traps, and many games and toys. Arranged under spring, summer, autumn and winter. The apparatus may be constructed of material easily obtained by almost any boy without cost, or by a very small outlay. Intended for the American boy who is "not too young to fly a kite or too old to enjoy a good day's fishing." Interest may be aroused in this kind of work by offering a prize for the best article made according to descriptions given in this book.

Chamberlain, J. F. How we are Sheltered

A geographical reader describing the houses of the cliff-dwellers, Indians, Japanese, Filipinos, etc., and with chapters on lumbering, the making of brick, artificial stone, nails and glass.

Goodrich, C. L. First Book of Farming

A good book for schools. The first part is a study of the general principles underlying plant culture and the second part is a study of soil fertility.

Sage and Cooley. Occupations for Little Fingers

A manual for grade teachers and mothers giving directions for papercutting, raffia work, sewing, weaving, clay modeling, etc.

BIOGRAPHY, DESCRIPTION, AND HISTORY

Eggleston, Edward. Stories of American Life and Adventure

Stories of Indian and frontier life, of adventures with pirates in colonial times, of daring feats in revolutionary times, and of scientific discoveries. A good supplementary reader that will interest boys especially.

Kelman, J. H. Stories from the Life of Christ

The stories are told in biblical language and the book itself is an attractive volume in good type with colored illustrations.

Tappan, E. M. American Hero Stories

Twenty-nine stories of makers of American history ranging from Columbus through Abraham Lincoln.

Carpenter, F. G. Asia

The record of a personally conducted tour of the Asiatic continent which is supposed to be made by every child who reads the book. The children travel over seas and lands, visit their little world brothers and sisters, see them at their work and their play, stay with them in their homes, and learn just how they live.

BOOKS FOR REFERENCE USE

Bryant, S. C. Stories to Tell to Children

Fifty-one stories with suggestions for telling.

Champlin, J. D. Young Folks' Cyclopedia of Persons and Places

See note under Champlin's Young Folks' Cyclopedia of Common Things on page 19. This volume gives the same information about persons and places that the other gives about common things. Both are needed if there is no other encyclopedia in the school.

Robbins, E. C. High School Debate Book

The best elementary book on debating. Gives valuable suggestions on how to debate, a model constitution and by-laws for a literary society, and briefs and references on 18 important political and social questions of the day.

SUPPLEMENTAL LIBRARY No. 2

Books Classified According to Subject

STORIES

Alcott, L. M. Old-fashioned Girl

Polly, a sensible little country girl, pays her first visit to a large city. As popular and almost as good as Little Women.

Cox, Palmer. Palmer Cox Brownie Primer

There are no more attractive picture books than the Brownie books of which there are six. But these books are expensive ($1.50 each) and do not wear very well. The Palmer Cox Brownie Primer is an excellent substitute and is always popular with the little children. Brownies swarm on every page intent on mischief and merrymaking, and stories, mostly in rhyme, accompany the pictures, but the illustrations are the important part.

Greene, Homer. Pickett's Gap
    A good railroad story that is very popular with the older boys.

Munroe, Kirk. Flamingo Feather
    A French boy's exciting adventures among the Spaniards and Florida Indians in the 16th century.

Seawell, M. E. Little Jarvis
    A navy story centering around the fight between the U. S. ship "Constellation" and the French frigate, "Vengeance."

Stoddard, W. O. Two Arrows
    A good Indian story which makes a strong plea for the education of the Indian.

MYTHS, FAIRY TALES, AND FABLES

Collodi, Carlo. Pinocchio
    An Italian story telling the adventures of a wooden marionette that endeavored to become a real boy.

Jacobs, Joseph. English Fairy Tales
    Contains more than a hundred of the old English fairy tales.

NATURE AND SCIENCE

Blanchan, Neltje. Birds That Every Child Should Know
    An attractive and interesting book on birds containing 72 photographs from life.

Kelly, Mrs. M. A. B. Short Stories of our Shy Neighbors
    Little nature studies describing in story fashion the form, color, and habits of various animals, birds and insects.

Long, W. J. Secrets of the Woods
    Stories of animal life which inspire love for animals and awaken an enthusiastic desire to study their habits and ways of life.

Stack, F. W. Wild Flowers Every Child Should Know
    Arranged according to color with descriptions of the more common species.

USEFUL ARTS

Chamberlain, J. F. How We are Fed
    A geographical reader describing the production and preparation for market of bread, meat, fish, rice, coffee, bananas and many other foods.

Morgan, Mrs. M. H. How to Dress a Doll
    Every process in making a doll's wardrobe is fully explained and when the clothes are all finished the child has acquired considerable skill in doing plain sewing.

BIOGRAPHY, DESCRIPTION, AND HISTORY

Connor and Poe. Life of Aycock
    Life of North Carolina's educational Governor and a collection of some of his best speeches.

Richards, Mrs. L. E. H. Florence Nightingale

By placing the emphasis upon the great and womanly qualities of the "Angel of the Crimea," this story of the life of Florence Nightingale plainly teaches that true greatness consists in nobility of character and service to others. An excellent biography for older girls.

Brooks, Dorothy. Stories of the Red Children

"What the little red children believe about the wind, stars, rain, and other natural phenomena. The type is large and the language simple."

Carpenter, F. G. South America

The relations of the United States with her southern neighbors are becoming very close and even the children should be more familiar with these countries. This geographical reader pictures the life and work of the people and describes the great industries of the various countries of South America.

Finnemore, John. Japan

An attractive book beautifully illustrated in color. Describes customs and life in Japan.

McDonald and Dalrymple. Kathleen in Ireland

A charming story giving information about Ireland and her people.

Poe, Clarence. A Southerner in Europe

Account of a visit to England, France, Belgium, Holland, Germany, Switzerland and Rome with a chapter on "How the South may win Leadership."

BOOKS FOR REFERENCE USE

Bacon, M. S. Songs Every Child Should Know

A collection of the best songs of all nations for young people.

Champlin, J. D. Young Folks Cyclopedia of Persons and Places

See note under Champlin's Young Folks' Cyclopedia of Common Things on page 19. This volume gives the same information about persons and places that the other gives about common things. Both are needed if there is no other encyclopedia in the school.

Repplier, Agnes. Book of Famous Verse

One of the best selected collections of poetry for children.

Lane and Hill. American History in Literature

A collection of prose and poetry dealing with the leading events of American history.

SUPPLEMENTAL LIBRARY No. 3

Books Classified According to Subject

STORIES

Aanrud, Hans. Lisbeth Longfrock

Charming story of life on a farm in Norway and of little Lisbeth Long-frock who reaches the height of her ambition when she becomes head milkmaid on the Hoel farm.

Montgomery, L. M. Anne of Green Gables

Anne is a lively, imaginative child from a Nova Scotia asylum who is adopted by an elderly farmer and his sister. A good school story, interesting to young girls and to most adults.

Porter, E. H. Pollyanna

Pollyanna, after the death of her father, a western missionary, goes to live with her aunt in Vermont. She takes with her the "glad game" which she had learned from her father, and not only plays it herself but persuades a great many others to play it with her. So Miss Polly's niece works a wonderful transformation in the community. Pollyanna is a book to read to old people, to sick people, and to young people, and whoever reads it or hears it read will be very likely to try to play the "glad game" too.

Potter, Beatrix. Tale of Benjamin Bunny

A delightfully illustrated book which will be very popular with the little children. It tells how Peter Rabbit lost his clothes and how Benjamin Bunny helped to find them.

Spyri, Johanna. Heidi

Heidi and her old grandfather lived in a hut in the Swiss Alps. She had many exciting experiences with Peter, a herd boy, and with a little girl from the city. The story is charmingly written and is one of the best for children in the intermediate grades. Good for reading aloud.

Stoddard, W. O. Red Mustang

A story of the Mexican border, telling how Cal Evans was captured by a band of Indians, and how Dick, the Red Mustang, saved his life.

Trowbridge, J. T. Tinkham Brothers' Tide Mill

"The successful fight of a family of boys to defend their rights and earn an honest living for their widowed mother, their sister and themselves. Mr. Trowbridge may not be a great writer, but he goes directly to the boyish heart."

Wiggin, Mrs. K. D. Rebecca of Sunnybrook Farm

Rebecca Rowena Randall goes from Sunnybrook Farm to live with her Aunt Mirandy, a hard, stern woman, who is to help her to an education which is to be the "making of her." The aunt fails to understand the fearless, honest, impulsive, beauty-loving child. The things which Rebecca does are enough to astonish less conservative people than Miss Miranda; but it would take a heart even harder than hers to steel itself against the child's charm. A fine wholesome story which big sister and mother will also enjoy.

MYTHS, FAIRY STORIES, AND FABLES

Andersen, H. C. Fairy Tales, edited by Turpin

A good collection for the younger children intended as a supplementary reader. The beautiful fairy tales of Andersen, although modern, have the true folklore spirit.

Norton, C. E. Heart of Oak Books. Volumes 1-2

The first book contains rhymes, jingles and fables; the second, fables and nursery tales.

Pyle, Howard. Some Merry Adventures of Robin Hood

Excellent abridgment of the author's larger and more expensive book ($3.00).

This is the book to give to boys who love adventure, for it tells "how in merry England in the times of old there lived within the green glades of Sherwood Forest a famous outlaw whose name was Robin Hood and

how he was attended by seven score yoeman bold who helped him in his
mad adventures."

SCIENCE AND AGRICULTURE

Noel, Maurice Buz; the Life of a Honey Bee

A lively story depicting the life and adventures of a honey bee. It is
good considered purely as a story and also has some value as natural
history.

Sargent, F. L. Corn Plants

Presents in an attractive way information regarding six of the most
important plants in the world—wheat, oats, rye, barley, rice and maize.
The book is intended as a supplementary reader, but it can also be used
to advantage in the preparation of teachers' talks.

BIOGRAPHY, DESCRIPTION, AND HISTORY

Kelly, M. D. Story of Sir Walter Raleigh

Sir Walter Raleigh is one of the favorite heroes of children, especially
of North Carolina children, and no wonder, for the story of his life is as
wonderful as any fairy tale. Hence this attractive little volume with
colored illustrations will be very popular.

Stone and Fickett. Everyday Life in the Colonies

Stories of early customs and celebrations. Useful for supplementary
reading with the United States history classes.

Carpenter, F. G. North America

The children, traveling through the United States, British America,
Mexico, and Central America, go through the cotton and tobacco plantations of the South, visit the orange groves of Florida, go down into
the mines, visit lumber camps and hunt for game. Mr. Carpenter knows
how to write for children and his Geographical readers are popular with
young people and indispensable for supplementary reading.

Connor and Poe. Life and Speeches of Charles Brantley Aycock

Life of North Carolina's educational Governor and a collection of some
of his best speeches.

Connor, R. D. W. Makers of North Carolina History

This book emphasizes the personalities of the great leaders of North
Carolina rather than the events in which they were concerned.

COLLECTIONS OF LITERATURE

Bryant, S. C. How to Tell Stories to Children

This is probably the best book for the inexperienced story-teller. It
discusses the purpose and uses of story telling in school, the selection
and adaptation of stories for telling, and how to tell the story. The last
half of the book contains 32 stories arranged according to grade, beginning with the kindergarten and extending through the fifth grade.

Cumnock, R. M. School Speaker

An excellent collection of recitations and speeches for the grades

Johnston and Barnum. Book of Plays for Little Actors

Very simple little plays for reading or acting in the primary grades.
Some of the plays are drawn from nursery classics and some are designed
for the celebration of special days.

Norton, C. E. Heart of Oak Books. Volumes 3-7

> Books three and four contain fairy stories, ballads and classic tales of adventure; books five, six and seven, masterpieces of literature. The selections in all seven volumes are chosen with special reference to the development of a taste for good reading and that is the reason these readers are included in this library.

BOOKS FOR REFERENCE USE

Champlin, J. D. Young Folks Cyclopedia of Common Things

> This little cyclopedia, covering natural science and useful arts, contains brief, simple articles that children can understand. It is also a valuable book for teaching the use of an encyclopedia, and hence it has a two-fold value in the rural school library.

ORIGINAL LIBRARY No. 1

Books Classified According to Grade

BOOKS FOR YOUNGEST READERS

Baldwin, James. Fairy Stories and Fables
Caldecott, Randolph. Picture Books. 2 Volumes
Grover, E. O. Overall Boys
Mother Goose. Book of Nursery Rhymes

BOOKS FOR INTERMEDIATE GRADES

Baldwin, James. Fifty Famous People
Brown, A. F. In the Days of Giants
Carroll, Lewis. Alice's Adventures in Wonderland
Eddy, S. J. Friends and Helpers
Greene, F. N. Legends of King Arthur and His Court
Grimm, J. L. & W. K. German Household Tales
Husted, M. H. Stories of Indian Chieftains
Jenks, A. E. Childhood of Ji-shib, the Ojibwa
Kingsley, Charles. Heroes; or Greek Fairy Tales for my Children
Kingsley, Charles. Water-babies
La Ramee, Louise de. The Dog of Flanders
Long, W. J. Ways of Wood Folk
Mulock, D. M. Little Lame Prince
Noel, Maurice. Buz; the life of a Honey Bee
Ruskin, John. King of the Golden River
Shaw, E. R. Big People and Little People of Other Lands
Spyri, Johanna. Heidi
Stevenson, R. L. Child's Garden of Verses
Stone and Fickett. Everyday Life in the Colonies

BOOKS FOR MORE ADVANCED STUDENTS

Alcott, L. M. Little Men
Alcott, L. M. Little Women.
Atkinson, G. F. First Studies of Plant Life
Bennett, John. Master Skylark

Benton, C. F. Saturday Mornings
Carpenter, F. G. Europe
Carpenter, F. G. How the World is Fed
Carpenter, F. G. North America
Connor and Poe. Life and Speeches of Charles Brantley Aycock
Defoe, Daniel. Robinson Crusoe
Duncan, Norman. Adventures of Billy Topsail
Harris, J. C. Uncle Remus; his Songs and Sayings
Hawthorne, Nathaniel. Wonder Book for Girls and Boys
Hughes, Thomas. Tom Brown's School Days
Jackson, H. H. Nelly's Silver Mine
Jewett, F. G. Good Health
Kelly, M. D. Story of Sir Walter Raleigh
Kipling, Rudyard. Jungle Book
Lamb, Charles and Lamb, Mary. Tales from Shakespeare
Miller, Mrs. O. T. First Book of Birds
Pyle, Howard. Some Merry Adventures of Robin Hood
Scudder, H. E. George Washington
Starr, Fredrick. American Indians
Stevenson, R. L. Treasure Island
Swift, Jonathan. Gulliver's Travels
Thompson, D. P. Green Mountain Boys
Wiggin and Smith. Golden Numbers
Wiggin, Mrs. K. D. Rebecca of Sunnybrook Farm
Williamson, Mrs. M. L. Life of General Robert Lee

BOOKS FOR REFERENCE USE

Champlin, J. D. Young Folks' Cyclopedia of Common Things
Johnston and Barnum. Book of Plays for Little Actors
Wiggin and Smith. Story Hour

ORIGINAL LIBRARY No. 2
Books Classified According to Grade
BOOKS FOR YOUNGEST READERS

Alderman, E. A. Classics Old and New. Volumes 1-2
Andersen, H. C. Fairy Tales, edited by Turpin
Baldwin, James. Fairy Reader
Grover, E. O. Sunbonnet Babies' Primer
Mother Goose. Book of Nursery Rhymes
O'Shea, M. V. Six Nursery Classics
Potter, Beatrix. Tale of Benjamin Bunny

BOOKS FOR INTERMEDIATE GRADES

Aanrud, Hans. Lisbeth Longfrock
Aesop. Child's Version of Aesop's Fables
Alderman, E. A. Classics Old and New. Volumes 3-5
Arabian Nights. Stories from the Arabian Nights
Baldwin, James. Old Greek Stories
Bayliss, C. K. Lolami, the Little Cliff Dweller

Bradish, S. P. Old Norse Stories
Brown. K. L. Plant Baby and Its Friends
Carroll, Lewis. Alice's Adventures in Wonderland
Eggleston, Edward. Stories of Great Americans for Little Americans
Francillon, R. E. Gods and Heroes
Fultz, F. M. The Flyaways and Other Seed Travelers
Husted, M. H. Stories of Indian Children
Lang, Andrew. Blue Fairy Book
Morley, M. W. Bee People
Mulock, D. M. Adventures of a Brownie
Ruskin, John. King of the Golden River
Sewell, Anna. Black Beauty
Stoddard, W. O. Red Mustang

BOOKS FOR MORE ADVANCED STUDENTS

Alcott, L. M. Little Men
Alcott, L. M. Little Women
Baker, R. S. Boys' Book of Inventions
Blaisdell and Ball. Hero Stories from American History
Bunyan, John. Pilgrim's Progress
Carpenter, F. G. Africa
Carpenter, F. G. North America
Connor, R. D. W. Makers of North Carolina History
Cooper, J. F. Last of the Mohicans
Defoe, Daniel. Robinson Crusoe
Dodge, Mrs. M. M. Hans Brinker
Guerber, H. A. Story of the Thirteen Colonies
Hawthorne, Nathaniel. Wonder Book for Girls and Boys
Jewett, S. O. Betty Leicester
Keller, Helen. Story of My Life
Montgomery, L. M. Anne of Green Gables
Mulock, D. M. John Halifax, Gentleman
Pier, A. S. Harding of St. Timothy's
Porter, E. H. Pollyanna
Roberts, C. G. Kindred of the Wild
Sargent, F. L. Corn Plants
Starr, Frederick. Strange Peoples
Stevenson, R. L. Treasure Island
Tappan, E. M. European Hero Stories
Trowbridge, J. T. Tinkham Brothers' Tide Mill
Wiggin, Mrs. K. D. Birds Christmas Carol
Wiggin, Mrs. K. D. Polly Oliver's Problem
Wyss, J. D. Swiss Family Robinson
Zollinger, Gulielma. Widow O'Callaghan's Boys

BOOKS FOR REFERENCE USE

Cumnock, R. M. School Speaker
Johnston and Chapin. Home Occupations for Boys and Girls
Lyman, Edna. Story Telling
Robbins, E. C. High School Debate Book
Stevenson, B. E. Days and Deeds: a Book of Verse

SUPPLEMENTAL LIBRARY No. 1

Books Classified According to Grade

BOOKS FOR YOUNGEST READERS

Cox, Palmer. Palmer Cox Brownie Primer
Scudder, H. E. Book of Fables
Wiltse, S. E. Folklore Stories and Proverbs

BOOKS FOR INTERMEDIATE GRADES

Carroll, Lewis. Through the Looking-glass
Chamberlain, J. F. How We are Sheltered
Eggleston, Edward. Stories of American Life and Adventure
Kelman, J. H. Stories from the Life of Christ
Morley, M. W. Seed Babies
Segur, S. R. Story of a Donkey
Tappan, E. M. American Hero Stories

BOOKS FOR MORE ADVANCED STUDENTS

Alcott, L. M. Jo's Boys
Beard, D. C. What to do and How to do it; the American Boys' Handy Book
Carpenter, F. G. Asia
Dickens, Charles. Christmas Carol and the Cricket on the Hearth
Dix, B. M. Merrylips
Ewing, J. H. Jackanapes
Gibson, W. H. Blossom Hosts and Insect Guests
Goodrich, C. L. First Book of Farming
Hawthorne, Nathaniel. Tanglewood Tales
Inman, Henry. Ranch on the Oxhide
Porter, G. S. Laddie
Seton, E. T. Rolf in the Woods

BOOKS FOR REFERENCE USE

Bryant, S. C. Stories to Tell to Children
Champlin, J. D. Young Folks' Cyclopedia of Persons and Places
Robbins, E. C. High School Debate Book
Sage and Cooley. Occupations for Little Fingers

SUPPLEMENTAL LIBRARY No. 2

Books Classified According to Grade

BOOKS FOR YOUNGEST READERS

Brooks, Dorothy. Stories of the Red Children
Cox, Palmer. Palmer Cox Brownie Primer

BOOKS FOR INTERMEDIATE GRADES

Chamberlain, J. F. How We Are Fed
Collodi, Carlo. Pinocchio
Jacobs, Joseph. English Fairy Tales

Kelly, Mrs. M. A. B. Short Stories of Our Shy Neighbors
Long, W. J. Secrets of the Woods
McDonald and Dalrymple. Kathleen in Ireland
Morgan, Mrs. M. H. How to Dress a Doll

BOOKS FOR MORE ADVANCED STUDENTS

Alcott, L. M. Old-fashioned Girl
Blanchan, Neltje. Birds That Every Child Should Know
Carpenter, F. G. South America
Connor and Poe. Life and Speeches of Charles Brantley Aycock
Finnemore, John. Japan
Greene, Homer. Pickett's Gap
Munroe, Kirk. Flamingo Feather
Poe, Clarence. A Southerner in Europe
Richards, Mrs. L. E. H. Florence Nightingale
Seawell, M. E. Little Jarvis
Stack, F. W. Wild Flowers Every Child Should Know
Stoddard, W. O. Two Arrows

BOOKS FOR REFERENCE USE

Bacon, M. S. Songs Every Child Should Know
Champlin, J. D. Young Folks' Cyclopedia of Persons and Places
Lane and Hill. American History in Literature
Repplier, Agnes. Book of Famous Verse

SUPPLEMENTAL LIBRARY No. 3

Books Classified According to Grade

BOOKS FOR YOUNGEST READERS

Andersen, H. C. Fairy Tales, edited by Turpin
Norton, C. E. Heart of Oak Books. Volumes 1-2
Potter, Beatrix. Tale of Benjamin Bunny

BOOKS FOR INTERMEDIATE GRADES

Aanrud, Hans. Lisbeth Longfrock
Noel, Maurice. Buz; the Life of a Honey Bee
Norton, C. E. Heart of Oak Books. Volumes 3-7
Spyri, Johanna. Heidi
Stoddard, W. O. Red Mustang
Stone and Fickett. Everyday Life in the Colonies

BOOKS FOR MORE ADVANCED STUDENTS

Carpenter, F. G. North America
Connor and Poe. Life and Speeches of Charles Brantley Aycock
Connor, R. D. W. Makers of North Carolina History
Kelly, M. D. Story of Sir Walter Raleigh
Montgomery, L. M. Anne of Green Gables
Porter, E. H. Pollyanna

Pyle, Howard. Some Merry Adventures of Robin Hood
Sargent, F. L. Corn Plants
Trowbridge, J. T. Tinkham Brothers' Tide Mill
Wiggin, Mrs. K. D. Rebecca of Sunnybrook Farm

BOOKS FOR REFERENCE USE

Bryant, S. C. How to Tell Stories to Children
Champlin, J. D. Young Folks' Cyclopedia of Common Things
Cumnock, R. M. School Speaker
Johnston and **Barnum.** Book of Plays for Little Actors

HOW TO USE THE SCHOOL LIBRARY

Some one has said that there is no more important factor in our whole educational system, outside of the teacher, than a judiciously selected and widely used school library.

The use that is made of a school library depends largely, if not entirely, upon the teacher. If the teacher does not supervise her pupils' reading, if she makes no effort to direct it, if she herself does not love good books, the library will not be a very important factor in the school.

To successfully direct the reading of children, the teacher must possess certain qualifications. In the first place she must know children's books and she must know them thoroughly. She must have read the books in the school library, not ten or fifteen years ago, but recently, so that she can readily recall characters and incidents in the best and most important ones. Human nature is much the same in children as in grown people. We like to read what other people are reading and talking about, and so do children. If a friend tells us of a book which she is reading, or has read recently, and relates an incident or describes a character in an entertaining way, we are very likely to read that book if we can possibly get hold of it. But if, on the other hand, some one says: "Oh, yes; I've read such-and-such a book, but it was years ago, and I've almost forgotten it; I liked it then, but I hardly think I'd care much about it now," we have no desire to read the book. And so it is with children. To show unfamiliarity with the books we are trying to get the children to read or to adopt a superior attitude towards children's literature, will make it impossible for us to influence their reading to any great extent.

In the second place the teacher must be able to adapt books to the individual. This requires a sympathetic understanding of child nature. Very soon in our efforts to direct children's reading, we realize that, although we can lead a child to a good book, we can not make him read it. Many children have very definite ideas as to what they want to read and some, much to our discouragement, insist upon reading a very poor class of books. There are hundreds of boys who read Alger and Optic and will not read "Treasure Island" or "Tom Brown," and there are hundreds of girls who demand silly and sentimental love stories and impatiently cast aside the books we know they ought to read. The reason is clear. These boys and girls are seeking a definite current of thought which they find in one class of books and do not find in another. Tom Brown is not the hero the boy wants to be and Tom the Bootblack is; Rebecca is not the ideal of the girl but the lovely Lady Arabella is. To get this type of boy and girl to read a better class of books we must give them books which have the same keynote, books in which the action is very much the same, but the English better and the motive higher.

Another and most important essential is for the teacher to love books and to let the children see that she does. This love of books cannot be taught; some one has said that it must be caught. It is very easy to detect a book lover by the way he picks up a book, opens it, examines it, and lays it down. We need not always be talking about the care of books until the children are afraid to handle a school library book; but if we are always careful to place a book on a table or desk instead of pitching it aside, never to mark or turn down the pages and to open it in such a way that its back will not be permanently injured—in short, to treat books with respect, even text-books, the majority of the class will unconsciously treat them in the same way and will come to regard books as friends and valuable possessions and not as necessary evils. This is another instance in which example is better than precept.

And finally, the teacher must have an abiding faith in the power of books to impart ideas, to build character, to give pleasure, and to inspire high ideals. The teacher who thus appreciates the power and influence of books will realize that the greatest thing the school can do for the child, is to send him out into the world equipped with the ability and the desire to get ideas from the printed page and with a genuine love of good literature.

The purpose of the rural school library is threefold: It should enable children to form the reading habit and to cultivate a taste for good litera-ture; it should provide supplementary reading; and it should stimulate the intellectual life of the community. These objects were kept carefully in mind when the books were selected for the original libraries and the supple-mental libraries and an attempt made to include in each a few books of real literature, a few for supplementary reading and a few that the fathers and mothers and the big brothers and sisters would read and enjoy.

There are certain books a child should read while he is yet a child and these books should be in every school library. Hence, as many as possible were included in the Original $30.00 Libraries. The most important are Mother Goose, Alice's Adventures in Wonderland, Treasure Island, Swiss Family Robinson, Tom Brown's School Days, Aesop's Fables, Andersen's Fairy Tales, Arabian Nights, Grimm's Fairy Tales and Miss Alcott's stories. It is better for the child, whether he goes to the little country school or the big city school, to read, to be familiar with, to love these classics than to read all the so-called supplementary books in the language. The latter give information and are needed in every school but the former enlarge and enrich the child's life and probably help more than anything else to cultivate a taste for the best literature. Therefore the first thing for the teacher to do who is really interested in her pupils' reading, is to read again Aesop's Fables, Alice's Adventures, Mother Goose, Tom Brown, and all the others, and by example and precept encourage her pupils to read them also.

CLASSIFICATION OF THE BOOKS

That the teacher may know how to get the most out of every book and to give the right book to the right boy and girl at the right time the books in all five libraries are classified in two different ways. In the first list the books are classified according to subject matter; that is, all books treating of the same or similar subjects have been grouped under that subject. In the second list the books are arranged according to grade: Books for Youngest Readers, Books for Intermediate Grades, and Books for More Advanced Students. A few books have been listed under the heading, Books for Reference Use. A reference book is one which is not intended to be read through but to be consulted for definite information—the Champlin encyclopedias, for example. Books on story telling, Sage & Cooley's Occu-pations for Little Fingers, and other books suitable for teachers and parents to use with children are listed with the reference books.

In the lists classified according to subject a descriptive note is given under each title, and much useful information will be overlooked if the notes are not carefully read. That the teacher may fully understand the classification used we give below the general characteristics of the best books in the several classes and a brief discussion of the value of each class of books in the school room and in the child's development.

STORIES

Very few stories written for children are actually vicious, but many are poor, weak and undesirable. An unlimited supply of stories which have few good qualities, even though they have no harmful tendencies, will not make for high ideals and noble ambitions; and they will certainly destroy the child's love for the best literature.

"What we wish to reject are those luke-warm books so weak in their portrayal of good and so equally weak in their portrayal of wrong that they leave no impressions behind them; also those improbable stories sometimes thrilling, sometimes sentimental, and the tales of criminal adventure and excitement which have no place whatsoever. For the misinterpretations of life acquired through inferior juvenile reading hinder in varying degree the development which we seek, while on the other hand it is difficult to measure the influence for good which early reading may have in imparting to the child standards and ideals which will result in better citizenship."

The teacher who is familiar with the best children's stories will never ask why she must not give Alger and Optic to the boy and Elsie Dinsmore to the girl; for the teacher who knows the Alcott books, "Rebecca of Sunnybrook Farm," "Anne of Green Gables," "Nelly's Silver Mine," and a few others, will have a standard by which to measure all other stories for girls; and if she has read "Tom Brown's School Days," "Robinson Crusoe," and "Treasure Island," she will have a similar standard by which to judge boys' books.

The boy likes the tales of adventure, of outdoor sports, and animal life; the girl prefers the home story or the school story. Few boys will read stories written especially for girls, but many girls like boy's books. This interest should be encouraged, for girls who read vigorous, healthy stories of boy life will not care for the sickening sentimentality of the Elsie books nor the false sentiment of the trashy novel. But a different type of girl will not read boys' books; she wants home stories and revels in the pathetic tale. "Little Women" is, of course, the ideal American home story and it has never been surpassed, but "Rebecca of Sunnybrook Farm" and "Anne of Green Gables" are also good stories of this type.

It is necessary to watch the girl who craves the sad story, for she may read too many and become morbid. "Little Jarvis," "Jackanapes," and "Little Lame Prince" are excellent stories of this class.

The dividing line between juvenile and adult books is the love story. The boy will tolerate a little romance in the tale of adventure but he does not want just a simple love story. When he stops reading children's books he begins reading detective stories. The average girl, however, when she reaches her teens, demands the love story. She wants to read about romantic things that happen to other girls and that might happen to her. Then give her the love stories of Shakespeare and Chaucer, give her "John Halifax" and the novels of Scott, Dickens and Thackeray, and keep her reading the classic love story and the standard novels as long as you possibly can. Thus she will learn to love the best literature and to distinguish between real sentiment and false.

MYTHS, FAIRY STORIES, FABLES

Mother Goose and Picture Books constitute the child's first reading. Then come the fable, the fairy story and the myth. The simplest fables and fairy tales can be given him at a very early age and are much better than most of the primers and first readers that are often used. Both the fairy tale and the fable appeal to the child's fondness for animals and teach the difference between right and wrong on broad lines. People and animals are either good or bad and punishment is meted out to the latter as surely and as speedily as rewards are bestowed on the former. Hence fables and fairy stories appeal to and satisfy the child's sense of justice.

The child enjoys the myth as he would a poetic fairy tale, and takes little or no account of its symbolic meaning. The value of this class of literature in a child's development has sometimes been questioned but it is now generally conceded that he should be given the best versions of the mythological tales as soon as he is able to read them. They develop his appreciation of beauty and awaken his awe and reverence. Moreover, myths have furnished the subject of much of the world's great literature, painting, sculpture, music and drama. Hence an acquaintance with Greek, Roman and Scandinavian mythology is absolutely essential.

"Literature for Children," a book by Mr. Orton Lowe, contains the following excellent paragraph on the reading of the classic myths:

"The charm of the myths of Greek and Roman literature is enduring, because they embody both truth and beauty—sometimes held to be one and the same. Nothing but a perverted taste, that is fed on the prosaic processes of material achievements or the artificial standards of a moral system, could fail to find pleasure and inspiration in them. Their appeal is artistic, to the sense of beauty. Their truth is a deification of the longings of the human heart as it seeks for comfort and protection in a world whose mysterious events can hardly be fathomed. And their gods and heroes embody the great virtues that marked a classic people as much as they did the beauty of their intellectual achievements—the virtues of courage, patience, honor, loyalty, contentment. A normal disposition will take satisfaction in this interpretation of truth and beauty. Not only will its possessor be satisfied, but he will be ennobled by the very presence of these qualities before his keen senses. The world will seem to him more than a place in which he is to toil and spin day after day; his soul will dwell apart on a mountain where not all mortals can ever climb, a mountain crowded with culture. He can temporarily leave the common crofts, seek his solace and confession, and be all the better to ply again his allotted task. He will learn of one spot where the greed and brutality of industrial progress can not set its heel and leave the print of what is practical and ugly."

The "Wonderbook" and "Tanglewood Tales" give us the best version of the Greek mythological stories for children who have a large vocabulary and read easily, but for the younger children, Baldwin's "Old Greek Stories" and Francillon's "Gods and Heroes" are better. For Greek stories which inspire hero worship we must go to Kingsley's "Heroes."

The cycle of tales that have grown up around the name of King Arthur are the finest legends we can give a child, not only on account of their beauty and interest, but also because of their wondrous spirit of chivalry. A cheap and good edition is Greene's "King Arthur and His Court," listed in Original Library Number 1.

The old German folk tales have been charmingly retold by Grimm, and there is no better collection of the English fairy tales than the volumes edited by Joseph Jacobs.

The many volumes of fairy tales edited by Andrew Lang, vary greatly in merit. Some are good and some have no place in a children's collection. The best are the "Yellow Fairy Book," the Blue, the Red, and the Green.

There is usually a vast difference between the old and modern fairy tales. The old writers believed, the modern only make-believe, but the beautiful modern fairy tales of Hans Andersen have the true folklore spirit. Two excellent modern fairy tales are "The Little Lame Prince" and Ruskin's "King of the Golden River."

NATURE AND SCIENCE

We come now to what may be called books of information. These are the books which supplement the work of the class-room and many of them are designed for supplementary readers. Under this head come books of science, useful arts, and biography, travel and history.

Most children's books classed as science come under the head of nature books; that is, books about trees, stars, birds, plants, and animals. The group includes many undesirable books, but the best enlarge the child's knowledge of natural history, teach him to be observant, and inculcate a love for the great out-of-doors. A few of the best have been included in these libraries.

USEFUL ARTS

Useful arts include books explaining the practical application of scientific principles and those telling how to make and do things. Books in this class are numerous and excellent and are always very popular with boys. Baker's "Boy's Book of Inventions" is a good example. But boys of a mechanical turn of mind outgrow such books after a time and should then be encouraged to read the less technical adult books and especially the Scientific American.

Beard's "American Boys' Handy Book," Benton's "Saturday Mornings," and other books written to develop the child's mechanical skill and to direct his play instincts not only teach him to amuse himself but how to do things that are useful and worth while.

BIOGRAPHY, HISTORY, TRAVEL

A very important class of books deals directly with men and countries. These are books about people (biographies), books about what groups of men have done (histories), and books about the countries in which men live and travel (travel).

The lives of many famous men and women, although important and interesting, do not furnish examples for imitation, and biographies of this kind for children should be written in such a way as not to confuse the reader's moral values. Historical biography is valuable in so far as it shows the spirit and customs of other times and helps to fix the events of a particular period in the mind of a child. But young people should also have the lives of men and women of sterling character and noble ambitions as an example and an inspiration. Biographies like Richards' "Florence Nightingale" and Keller's "Story of My Life" have the highest ethical value.

Children will read biography that has a strong story interest and that furnishes an incentive for materializing their own dreams. The ideal juvenile biography teaches unconsciously; it does not erect "so-you-see" finger-posts but allows the reader to draw his own lessons and to make his own applications.

HISTORY

The following extracts are from an article on "Histories for Children," written by Miss Josephine A. Rathbone and published in the North Carolina Library Bulletin for March, 1912:

"But what may history do for the child? Its value, it seems to me, quite aside from the incidental one of conveying facts to his mind (a process dubiously termed 'improving'), is chiefly to stimulate imagination, to awaken admiration for the noble and heroic, to broaden his horizon by pictures of life under conditions foreign to his own experience. If this be the value of histories for children, it follows that the histories to be given to them are those that are dramatic, that tell a story and tell it vividly and well. The child who learns from Roman history to glory in the heroism of Horatius, to rejoice at the downfall of the Tarquins, who has been thrilled at the leap of Curtius—that child is richer far than though he knew every date from the founding of the city to its fall. The fact that the stories are true only intensifies the interest, but it is primarily as stories that history has its value for children. Therefore, while it is well that the facts in the children's histories agree with those established by recent scholarship, yet that is after all a secondary consideration, and many of the old favorites, though they may present as historical events that have since been pronounced to be mere legend, are really valuable because readable and of human interest, true to human nature if not to historical fact. . . . . Young children have little conception of time or chronology; last week, or at most, last year, is as far back as they can conceive, so it is not possible for them to hold in their minds an historic frame-work or skeleton of centuries; that will come later and things will fit themselves into it gradually. In the meantime let them acquire an interest in real people and in real things, or rather try and make these things and people real to them.

"Therefore let the librarian select for children's reading, books that are interesting, that emphasize noble qualities shown in the heroic past, and let her aim to stimulate patriotism while avoiding the perpetuation of antagonism and prejudice."

Guerber's "Story of the Thirteen Colonies," Tappan's "European Hero Stories," and Stone and Fickett's "Everyday Life in the Colonies" are readable and full of human interest and this is their chief value. Incidentally the child who reads them is becoming familiar with the manners and customs of the early settlers, is learning a great deal about the people of the thirteen original colonies and is getting a good background for the study of American history.

TRAVEL

The reading of descriptions of our own and other countries is one of the best ways of making geography a live subject; it adds ideas about social life and customs, atmosphere and local color to the plain and usually uninteresting statements of facts contained in the text-books. Unfortunately books of travel are less interesting to children than almost any other class. This is probably because they do not deal so directly with people and because few juvenile books of travel have any real value. But interest can usually be awakened in books describing child life in other lands and in those containing more adventure than description. The Carpenter geographical readers are probably the best books of travel for young people and at least one is included in each library. "Kathleen in Ireland" and some of the other volumes belonging to the Little People Everywhere series, Finnemore's "Japan," one of the books in the Peeps at Many Lands series, and Shaw's "Big People and Little People" are also good.

COLLECTIONS OF LITERATURE

Under this head poetry, plays, readers and speakers, and books on debating and story telling will be discussed.

When children are young is the time to develop a taste for the best poetry. Nearly all children love poetry naturally; that is, they like to hear a great poem well read even if they do not enjoy reading it to themselves. The poem which is musical and simple in thought and construction is the poem which will make the strongest appeal.

There are some excellent collections of poetry for children. These contain poetry written especially for them and a great deal written for adults but liked by children. For the youngest children Robert Louis Stevenson's "Child's Garden of Verses" and the poems in the first two or three volumes of the "Heart of Oak Books" and of "Classics Old and New" are recommended. For the older children Mrs. Wiggin's "Golden Numbers" and Miss Repplier's "Book of Famous Verse" are excellent collections.

Children are dramatic by nature and teachers are beginning to utilize this dramatic instinct in the work of the class-room. Dramatic reading is a means of training the imagination and of quickening literary appreciation. The child who has had good training in dramatization talks intelligently and expresses himself well; he is not shy when meeting strangers nor afflicted with stage fright if he appears in a public entertainment. If the reading lesson or the history lesson is sometimes dramatized the interest is increased a hundredfold.

"A Book of Plays for Little Actors," by Johnston and Barnum, is in Original Library Number 1 and Supplemental Library Number 3. It gives simple little plays to be used in the primary grades and after the children have read and acted them they can with a little help from the teacher adapt other nursery classics in the same way. The Library Commission has a collection of plays for school use, some of them founded on historical events or personages, and the Commission will be glad to lend them without charge to any rural school in North Carolina.

In recent years there has been a revival of interest in both debating and story telling and teachers have felt the need of books dealing with both subjects. Robbins' "High School Debate Book" is the best volume on this subject for beginners and the teacher can find no more helpful books on story telling than Miss Bryant's "Stories to Tell to Children" and "How to Tell Stories to Children." Miss Lyman's "Storytelling; What' to Tell and How to Tell It," gives excellent material for use with the older children.

CYCLOPEDIAS

Every school needs a good encyclopedia, but a poor one is a very bad investment. The best for general use is the New International Encyclopedia, published by Dodd Mead & Company and sold at $5.00 per volume (21 volumes). Few schools, however, can afford such an expensive work, and Appleton's New Practical Cyclopedia is excellent for school use. It is in six volumes and although published at $18.00 it can now be secured for $9.75.

The Champlin cyclopedias can be most highly recommended and are almost indispensable in the grammar grades even if the school has one of the more comprehensive encyclopedias. This is the reason they are included in four of the rural school libraries. The "Young Folks' Cyclopedia of Common Things" covers natural science and useful arts and the "Young Folks' Cyclopedia of Persons and Places" covers persons and events. Hence one supplements the other and both are really necessary. By using these books a child acquires the habit of looking up things and learns how to find what he wants, and later he will not have any trouble in using the more elaborate cyclopedias.